my book of firsts

with Sophie la girafe®

my book of firsts
with Sophie la girafe®

THE EXPERIMENT
NEW YORK

Contents

The book lists your child's firsts in chronological order. But here we've listed them by theme to help you find the one you want!

Activities
First peekaboo 29
First trip to the park 44
First time on a merry-go-round 45
First trip to the zoo 53
First time at the pool 55
First trip to the beach 56
First time in a lake or the ocean 57
First time on stage 90
First trip to the movies 91
First extracurricular activity 92

Care and Health
First check-up 10
First bath 18
First visit to the pediatrician 24
First tooth 48
First boo-boo 60
First illness 61
First haircut 68
First lost tooth 94

Clothes
First outfit 12
First shoes 13
First time getting dressed alone 82
First favorite outfit 83

Diapers and Potty Training
First diaper change 14
First accident during a diaper change 30
First overflowing diaper 31
First time on the potty 76
First night without a diaper 77

Discoveries

First music 36
First animal 37
First snow 51
First summer 54
First favorite book 70
First favorite toy 71
First drawing 72
First favorite movie or show 85
First stick figure 86

Emotions

First cries 9
First smile 20
First bout of colic 25
First pacifier or thumb-sucking 26
First blankie or lovey 28
First laugh 33
First tantrum 75

Food

First feeding 11
First time in a high chair 39
First solid foods 40
First taste experiments 42
First sweet treat 43
First time eating independently 64

Independence

First time grabbing 32
First time turning over 35
First time sitting up 38
First time with a babysitter 47
First time crawling 49
First time standing up alone 59
First steps 65
First time climbing stairs 74
First tricycle 79

Language

First babbles 34
First word 69
First nursery rhyme 78
First "signature" 88

Love

First time seeing your baby 8
First time at home 15
First holiday 50
First kiss from baby 58
First birthday 67

Sleep

First night in the crib 19
First time sleeping through the night 46
First night apart 62
First night in a "big kid" bed 84

Social life

First time meeting the family 16
First time meeting family friends 17
First time at daycare 63
First friend 66
First "big kid" birthday party 80
First day at school 87
First school field trip 89
First sleepover 95

Travel

First time in a baby carrier or sling 21
First time in a stroller 22
First car ride 23
First big trip 52

First times are filled with many emotions. Part of the joy of being a parent is marveling at each milestone in your child's life. As your child grows and learns, your role is to help, support, encourage, and reassure during the many exciting steps and events along the way.

Use this book to record and remember all of these precious moments. From the first smile to the first sleepover, from tender moments to things that made you laugh out loud, you can keep track of every detail of your child's early years.

When your child grows up and starts a new chapter in life, this book will give you a treasure trove of memories to look back on and relive.

First time seeing your baby

You'll never forget the first time you laid eyes on this little person after all those months of waiting. From that moment on, your bundle of joy will always be in your thoughts . . .

Date ....

Place .... Time ....

How did you feel? ....

....

....

....

....

How did your baby look (calm, happy, angry, sulky, focused, etc.)? ....

....

....

First cries

Whether the roar of a lion or the mew of a kitten,
your baby's first cry was the sound of your new life
together and a fond memory you'll always cherish.

When did your baby cry for the first time? ....

....

Were you able to calm your baby down quickly?

....

....

....

What were your first words to your baby?

....

....

....

....

First check-up

Soon after delivery, your baby's hearing and heart were tested, and some blood was taken to assess her health. This was your baby's first "ouch" moment in a long line of check-ups and booster shots to come . . .

Your baby's weight: ....

Your baby's length: ....

Tests run: ....
....
....

How did your baby react? ....
....
....
....

How did you feel during the check-up? ....
....
....
....

First feeding

Was your baby voracious or picky? Quickly satisfied or hungry all the time? A baby's first feeding experience is a major milestone in discovering his senses . . . and the world!

Breast or bottle? ....

When was the first time you fed him? ....

How did your baby do? Was he calm or agitated?

....

If you breastfed, what was it like? ....

....

....

If you bottle-fed, what kind of formula did you

use? ....

....

How much milk did your baby take? ....

....

....

First outfit

You probably spent hours picking out your baby's first clothes. Indeed, the first outfit can feel like a projection of your future child. Did you go for something classic or quirky?

Describe your baby's first outfit: ....

....

....

....

Who dressed her? ....

Add a photo of your baby
in her first outfit.

First shoes

Some parents buy baby shoes way in advance . . . for sure,
they're one of the cutest things to shop for! You'll soon
be buying shoes constantly as your child grows, but
these brand-new baby booties sure made you proud!

What size were the shoes? ....

What type of shoes were they? ....

....

What did they look like? ....

....

Who chose them? ....

....

Did your baby like wearing them? ....

....

....

....

....

First diaper change

The first of many, many to come, that initial diaper change makes potty training seem very far in the future! Until then, you'll become a diaper-changing expert.

How did you fare on the first attempt? Check the best answer:

- ○ With flying colors (secure diaper, calm baby, admiring looks from the nurse)
- ○ Could have done better (leaky diaper, fussy baby, shaky hands)
- ○ Catastrophe (diaper on backward, grumpy baby, and totally discouraged)

Who attempted the feat first? ....

....

Did you practice beforehand? ....

....

What kind of diapers did you use?

- ○ Disposable
- ○ Cloth

First time at home

What a joy to finally introduce baby to your home!
Get ready for some changes—you now have a new
roommate, who's going to turn your life upside down!

Date ....

What was the weather like? ....

....

....

....

Who carried baby inside? ....

....

....

How did you feel? ....

....

....

....

First time meeting the family

Your family waited anxiously for the big day! Grandpa and grandma, uncles and aunts, brothers and sisters all waited anxiously to "ooh" and "ah" over your bundle of joy.

Who came to visit? ....

....

....

Which touching remarks do you remember most?

....

....

What did people bring? ....

....

....

Precious memories: ....

....

....

....

First time meeting family friends

Another addition to the gang is always a reason to celebrate! You probably had people over to talk about the new person in your life, or maybe you made the rounds after things settled down a bit.

Who were your first friends to meet your baby?

....

....

....

....

Who made you laugh? Why? ....

....

....

....

Did anyone make you cry? Why? ....

....

....

First bath

Bath time is special for you and your baby: you get to know him from head to toe, touch that irresistibly soft skin, and cover him in kisses.

How did the first bath go? ....

....

....

Where did your baby take his first bath (baby tub, family bathtub, sink)? ....

....

Who gave the bath? ....

Were you nervous? ....

....

How did your baby react? ....

....

....

First night in the crib

You were probably anxious for your baby's first night
in the nest you had prepared for her in your home.
You couldn't wait to introduce her to her room,
her bed, and everything else!

What was your baby's reaction when you put her
down in her crib?..

....

....

How did you feel?.................................... ....

....

How did baby sleep? ....

....

Did your baby actually sleep in her own bed or
did she end up sleeping somewhere else?.......................

....

....

....

First smile

The first smile seems a long time coming.
You go through scads of diaper changes and feedings
with nothing in return. Then one day, it happens:
your baby smiles right at you. This symbol of well-being,
trust, and love makes all the work so worth it!

How old was your baby? ....

When did it happen? ....

....

....

Who was there? ....

....

....

How did it make you feel? ....

....

....

....

....

First time in a baby carrier or sling

It looks so simple when you see a mom carrying her baby in a sling or carrier on her chest, and you daydreamed about being hands-free while keeping your baby close. But that first attempt can be awkward. Which part goes over the shoulder? Where do baby's arms go? Best to just laugh as you keep your baby from falling out . . .

What carriers did you try? ....

....

How old was your baby? ....

Did someone "show you the ropes"? ....

....

How did it go on the first try? ....

....

....

What have you used since then? ....

....

First time in a stroller

You spent hours poring over websites and catalogs and browsing through stores to find the perfect stroller. Now it's time to take it out for a spin!

Did your baby like his first day on the town? ....

....

Where did you go? ....

Who pushed? ....

....

What kind of stroller was it? ....

....

Was it easy to manage? ....

....

Were you happy with your purchase? ....

....

....

First car ride

Learning how the car seat works, turning around every five seconds to make sure your baby is okay, wanting to scream at other drivers that you've got a baby on board . . . the first car ride can be a whirlwind adventure! How was it for you?

Date ....

You went from ....

    to ....

Did your baby like the trip? ....

....

....

How did you feel?...

....

....

Your car-seat satisfaction level:

    O Piece of cake

    O Everything got buckled

    O Worse than changing a diaper

First visit to the pediatrician

Your pediatrician is a great resource during those early childhood years! She'll listen to your problems (and share your joys), while reassuring, comforting, and supporting you. Over time, you'll get to know one another very well. What were your impressions that first visit?

How did you choose your doctor? ....
....

What was the experience like? ....
....

What was your first impression? ....
....

What good advice did she give? ....
....

How did your baby react? ....
....
....

First bout of colic

Day or night, it happens without warning: the dreaded colic.
No matter what you do, you just can't calm your screaming
baby. You feel powerless, which is okay. You may have to
let her cry it out while you hold her to comfort and soothe.
But how exhausting!

How old was your baby? Where did it start? ....

....

How long did it last? ....

....

What did you do to soothe your baby? ....

....

....

....

How did it make you feel? ....

....

....

....

First pacifier or thumb-sucking

Nothing calms a baby down faster than a pacifier or a finger to suck on. Although some may say your baby will become dependent on it, simply ask if they're the ones who'll be staying up at night to calm your fussy baby!

Did your child prefer a pacifier or a finger?

....

Pacifier

How old was your baby when you first gave him a pacifier? ....

Where were you? ....

....

How did your child react? ....

....

....

What was your child's name for it? ....

....

Did he soon need it all the time? ....

....

How did you convince him to give it up? ....

....

....

Thumb

At what age did your baby start sucking his

thumb or other finger? ....

Do you remember when you first noticed? ....

....

....

Did he do it frequently? ....

....

When did he grow out of it? ....

....

....

First blankie or lovey

Since her birth, your baby has received loads of soft blankets and stuffed animals. She probably picked a favorite from this mountain of cuddly objects, and it might not be the one you expected. You suddenly have a new member of the family that you can't leave home without!

When did your child first become attached to a favorite blanket or toy? ....

What did she call it? ....

What did it look like? ....

....

Who gave it to her? ....

....

Stories about your child's blankie or lovey: ....

....

....

....

First peekaboo

What is it about this simple game that babies love so much?
Once they know about it, you could spend hours "hiding"
from them! Were you as entertained as your baby was?

How old was your baby? ....

Where were you? ....
....

Who first played it with him? ....
....

How did your baby react? All smiles, or wide-eyed
in surprise? ....
....
....
....

What were some other favorite games? ....
....
....

First accident during a diaper change

Changing your baby is a time of togetherness. But you probably burst into tears (or laughter) the first time a stream appeared before the new diaper was in place! A quick change turned into a full-out cleaning of your child, changing pad, and onesie. Rest assured, you're not the first parent this has happened to . . . nor the last!

How old was your baby? ....

Were you alone? What was your reaction? ....

....

....

....

What tricks did you come up with to avoid it

happening again? ....

....

....

....

First overflowing diaper

Whether it happens at the park, at a restaurant, in the car, or at home, an overflowing diaper is always a nightmare! Do you start cleaning from the toes or head? How do you get the diaper off without getting the mess everywhere? Before you know it, you're as overwhelmed as baby!

How old was your baby? ....

Where did it happen the first time? ....

....

....

What was your initial thought? ....

....

....

Did you swear the diaper was defective? Did you change brands? Did you check your technique?

....

....

....

First time grabbing

It took a lot of concentration, furrowed eyebrows, and an inquisitive stare, but your baby finally did it: she grabbed her first object (a rattle, a spoon—maybe even Sophie la girafe)! Your baby has taken a big step in mastering the world around her. From now on, she won't stop exploring the world with her fingers! And you won't stop worrying about what those fingers will get into . . .

How old was your baby? ....

What did she grab? ....

....

Why did she want it? ....

....

....

Who was there? ....

....

....

....

First laugh

Your baby's laugh is one of the most treasured sounds there is. Just one little squeal and you can't help but giggle yourself. Sharing a laugh with your baby is a little thing that brings big joy!

How old was your baby? ....

Where were you? ....
....

Who was there? ....
....

What caused the laugh? ....
....
....

Did he laugh again right away? ....
....
....
....

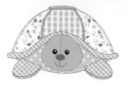

First babbles

Spending so much time with your baby, you get used to one-sided conversations. Then, suddenly one day, that first attempt at speaking escapes her lips, and you couldn't be more proud. Now that you've started the conversation, don't let it stop!

How old was your baby? ....

When did she first start babbling (after a meal, in your arms, in bed)? ....

....

....

Who was there? ....

....

....

What did you say back to her? ....

....

....

....

First time turning over

The first time your baby turns over, it means he's mastering his motor skills and on his way to learning to walk. Before you know it, he'll be learning his ABC's and 123's . . .

How old was your baby? ....

Where were you? ....

Did it happen before your eyes, or did you catch a glimpse from another room? ....
....
....

Did you encourage your baby to turn, or did he do it all by himself? ....
....
....

How did your child react? ....
....

Did he do it again right away? ....

....

First music

Lullabies or rock music? Classic or current?
A grand ensemble or an intimate acoustic?
What are the musical tastes of your little Mozart?

What was the first music (or song) you played for

your baby? ....

....

What was her reaction? ....

....

....

Did the music soothe her? ....

....

Did you try different musical genres? ....

....

What was her favorite music? ....

....

....

First animal

Your pet cat, a bird on the sidewalk, a cow in a field, or a giraffe at the zoo: your child's first contact with an animal is a world of wonder and amazement.

When did your child meet his first furry friend?

....

....

....

What kind of animal was it? ....

....

Any funny details to remember? ....

....

....

....

What is your child's favorite animal? ....

....

....

First time sitting up

After taking many tumbles and spills, your baby
finally discovered her balance and sat up straight.
The proof: you could leave her on the floor, and she
stayed put . . . for all of 5 seconds!

How old was your child when she reached this

milestone? ....

Was she proud of herself? ....

....

....

How did it make you feel? ....

....

....

Where were her favorite spots to sit? ....

....

....

....

First time in a high chair

Cribs, bouncers, and activity mats are now a thing
of the past: it's time for baby to graduate to the high chair!
Your little one is now old enough to sit up unassisted and
wants to be at table height to see what's going on.
Welcome to the big leagues!

How old was your child? ....

Did he like his chair? ....

....

....

....

What kind of chair was it? ....

....

What did the high chair change in your life? ....

....

....

....

....

First solid foods

How delightful to discover other flavors besides milk!
And so many surprises, too! When you got the green light
to introduce solid foods, which ones did you try first?

How old was your baby? ....

What was her reaction to the first bite? ....

....

....

How much did she eat the first time? ....

....

....

What was the first fruit she tried? ....

....

....

The first vegetable? ....

....

....

The first foods you introduced, and your child's reactions:

1. ....

2. ....

3. ....

4. ....

5. ....

6. ....

7. ....

8. ....

9. ....

10. ....

First taste experiments

There's nothing funnier than testing new foods on a new tongue: your baby's eyes widen in surprise, his nose wrinkles in disgust, or a big grin breaks out as he eagerly reaches for more.

Puréed spinach? Guava juice? What "flavor surprises" did you try on your baby? ....

....

....

How old was he? ....

His favorites? ....

....

His not-so-favorites? ....

....

Any surprising reactions? ....

....

....

First sweet treat

Giving your child something sugary-sweet for the first time may start her down a path of no return . . . Most likely your tiny tot will adore the taste, and you'll have to shell out more or learn to say no! Ah, the problem with the good things in life: they lead to both happiness and frustration . . .

How old was your child? ....

What did she have? ....

What was the occasion? ....

....

What was her reaction? ....

....

....

....

Did she ask for more? ....

....

....

First trip to the park

For your little monkey, the park is a new land of discovery and freedom. But you need a steady hand to guide and protect him. This is a new experience you'll continue to share again and again . . .

How old was your baby? ....

Which park did you go to? ....
....

How was it? ....
....

What was his favorite: the slide? the swings? something else? ....
....
....

When you had to leave, how did your baby react?
....
....
....

First time on a merry-go-round

The merry-go-round is a rite of passage for both children and parents—there's something special about watching your child as she goes round and round on a unicorn or elephant. (Although that first experience may be more fun for you than for her!)

How old was she? ....

Where was it? ....

....

Who was there? ....

....

What animal did your child ride? ....

....

What was her reaction? Did she want to keep going or get off? ....

....

....

First time sleeping through the night

After months of trying everything from letting your baby cry it out to going to look in on him every five minutes, it finally happened—he slept through the night! A feeding, a cuddle, a song, and voilà: he drifted off to sleep. It's a wonderful reward for all that work.

How old was your baby? ....

How did you do it? ....

....

....

....

....

For you, "sleeping through the night" meant how

many hours? ....

....

....

First time with a babysitter

From the beginning, you and your baby have spent day and night together as a single unit. Then one day, you have to leave your baby behind, just to get a breather or run some non-baby friendly errands. Leaving your little one behind is a big test on the road to separation.

How old was your baby? ....

Where did you go? ....

....

Who babysat? ....

How did you feel when you left? ....

....

How did your baby react? ....

....

How did you feel when you got home? ....

....

....

First tooth

One day your baby opens her mouth and you notice the beginnings of her first pearly white. It's a big milestone in your baby's life . . . now you just have to watch out for biting!

When did your baby get her first tooth? ....

....

What tooth was it? ....

How long did it take to come through? ....

....

How did your baby handle teething? ....

....

....

Did she have a favorite teething toy? ....

....

....

Any tricks for helping her through the pain? ....

....

....

First time crawling

It used to be so easy: you plopped your baby down and he stayed put. Now, you're constantly playing hide and seek!

How old was your baby? ....

Where was he the first time he crawled? ....

....

....

What did he want to get? ....

....

....

....

How was he at crawling? ....

....

....

....

....

First holiday

The first big holiday with your child is always emotional, even if the meaning is lost on her! But she'll soon take to the cheerful atmosphere, festive decorations, and heaps of attention from family and friends.

How old was your child? ....

What was the holiday? ....

How did you celebrate? ....

....

Special memories: ....

....

....

Add a photo from your child's first holiday.

First snow

A world transformed into soft, white landscapes that beg to be played in makes baby's first snow a true marvel for the senses!

How old was your child?..

Where were you?...

....

What did you do? ....

....

....

Add a photo from your
child's first snow.

First big trip

Whether by plane, train, or automobile, baby's first trip
is a big adventure! Bringing him along means bringing a
truckload of gear. You soon realize how much easier
it was to lug him around in your belly!

When? ....

Where did you go? ....

How did you get there? ....

....

What did you bring? ....

....

Did you forget anything? ....

....

How did the trip go? ....

....

....

First trip to the zoo

The first time you visit the zoo with your child, you can't get enough of her reactions to the animals! Look out Mr. Lion—someone has stolen your spotlight!

How old was your child? ....

Where was it? ....

....

Who joined your expedition? ....

....

What was your child's favorite animal? ....

....

....

Any funny anecdotes you want to remember?

....

....

....

First summer

Summer is full of warm, carefree days in cute bathing suits and bonnets. You get to take your baby on family outings and trips to enjoy the sun.

What did you and your baby do that first summer? ....

....

....

Who did you see and spend time with? ....

....

What places did you visit? ....

....

....

Favorite memories from that summer: ....

....

....

....

First time at the pool

A pool can be overwhelming for your child, but he probably
loved the sensation of moving freely in the water—especially
since you were there for safety!

How old was your child? ....

Where were you? ....

....

Who took a dip with him? ....

....

Did he have water wings or a flotation suit?

....

....

What was his reaction? ....

....

....

....

First trip to the beach

The early years of going to the beach with your child can be a challenge. She gets sand in her eyes, mouth, diaper—places you didn't think it could go! But once your baby realizes where the sand is supposed to stay, the beach becomes an exciting land of discovery!

How old was your child? ....

Where were you? ....

....

What was the weather like? ....

....

What did she do?..

....

Add a photo from your child's
first time at the beach.

First time in a lake or the ocean

The first time swimming in open water can be scary, with the cold water, big waves, slimy seaweed, and other unknowns. But when your baby first dips in his toe, the water becomes the most fascinating of toys!

How old was your baby? ....

....

Where was it? ....

....

Who held him? ....

....

How did he react? ....

....

....

Did he want to go back in? ....

....

First kiss from baby

You cover your baby with kisses, and then one day your baby turns around and gives you one right back! Whether it's a slobbery smooch, a loud smack, or a polite peck, this sign of affection makes your heart melt!

How old was your baby? ....

Who received the kiss? ....

....

What was the occasion? ....

....

....

What did it feel like? ....

....

....

Did your baby keep up the kissing? ....

....

....

First time standing up alone

After sitting and crawling, your child finally
figured out how to get vertical. Your child now tries
to get "up" by grabbing onto anything she can.
Watch out—and remember to toddler-proof everything!

When did you see your child stand up alone for
the first time? ....

....

....

What did she hold on to? ....

....

....

How successful was she at standing up? ....

....

....

How did you childproof your home? ....

....

....

First boo-boo

Your baby's exploration of the world means getting some bumps and bruises along the way—you just have to get used to it. Of course, ointment and bandages are magical at making those pesky boo-boos all better!

When did your baby get his first boo-boo? ....

....

....

What happened? ....

....

....

Where was the boo-boo? ....

....

Did he cry a lot? ....

....

How worried were you? ....

....

First illness

Although necessary for building immunity, childhood illnesses are tough times. All parents have had to deal with raging fevers, a cough that won't quit, and heart-rending cries you just can't soothe.

How old was your child? ....

What were the first symptoms? ....

....

What did the doctor say? ....

....

....

What was the treatment? ....

....

....

How long did it take for your child to get better?

....

....

First night apart

It feels a bit odd—an entire night without your child
by your side! A business trip, a romantic escapade, or
simply a chance to sleep . . . with the promise of not being
woken at 5:00 a.m.! Did you spend the night in peaceful
slumber, or did you toss and turn?

Who babysat? ....

How old was your child? ....

What was the occasion? ....

....

Were you stressed about leaving your child?

....

....

How did it go? ....

....

Were you able to relax? ....

....

First time at daycare

The period of early bonding for you and your baby has come
to an end. This transition is rough, but it's time to leave your
child with a nanny or daycare and get back to your adult life.
Now it's your child's turn to have her own experiences!

What type of childcare did you choose? ....

....

How old was your child? ....

How did your child react? ....

....

....

How did you react? ....

....

....

Did it take your child long to adapt? ....

....

....

First time eating independently

After what seems like a million mealtimes feeding your baby, it's time for her to finally try doing it on her own! There's nothing more exciting than watching your child take those first wobbly bites—even if it gets a little messy!

How old was your child? ....

Did she want to try, or did you decide it was

time? ....

....

....

What did she have? ....

....

....

How did it go? ....

....

....

....

First steps

The day has come! Your little one has found his footing! You're ecstatic, and he's feeling especially pleased with his new ability! These are his first steps into the big, wide world . . .

How old was your child? ....

Where did he take his first steps? ....

....

....

How did you encourage him? ....

....

....

After the first tumble, did he try standing up again right away, or was he a bit nervous? ....

....

....

....

First friend

A sandbox buddy, a stroller sidekick, or a
play-date pal: relationships can go way back!
Who was your child's official first friend?

His or her name? ....

....

When did they meet for the first time? ....

....

Did they play together often? ....

....

....

A memorable story from a play date: ....

....

....

Did they continue playing together as they grew?

....

....

First birthday

The birthday girl might not have blown out the first candle by herself; she was probably too excited about the hubbub all around. Even if you blew it out for her, you had reason to celebrate an entire year of joys and discoveries, and the many more to come . . .

Where did you celebrate the big day? ....

....

Who was there? ....

....

What gifts did she receive? ....

....

Add a photo from your
child's first birthday

First haircut

Your child changes so much: one day he's a baby,
the next he's a little boy. That first lock of fallen
hair is a new chapter in your child's life!

How old was your child? ....

Where did he get his first haircut? ....

....

Who did the honors? ....

....

How did your child react? ....

....

Add a photo from your
child's first haircut.

First word

Was it *da, da, da* ("You heard it, she said 'dada'!") or *ma, ma, ma* ("Uh-uh, she said 'mama'!")? As your baby "finds her voice," she discovers a whole new form of interaction, and you'll go nuts over all her cute new sounds.

When did your child start talking? ....

....

Who heard it first? ....

....

What did your child say? ....

....

....

....

How did her vocabulary evolve after that? ....

....

....

....

First favorite book

Try as you might to suggest another book, your child won't hear of it. Now that you've read the story for the 57th time, you feel like you could recite it in your sleep. But you still love how his favorite book brings you two together!

What was the title of your child's first must-read?

....

What was it about? ....

....

....

What did your child like in particular? ....

....

....

....

And you? ....

....

....

First favorite toy

Your child's first blankie or lovey will always hold a special place in her heart, but once she's a bit older and her sense of play really kicks into gear, you can't tear her away her favorite train set or building blocks, even at mealtime and bedtime!

What was your child's favorite toy to play with?

....

Where was her favorite place to play? ....

....

Did she play any creative games with her toy? ....

....

How old was she when you first noticed her attachment to this one toy? ....

Any funny stories?...

....

....

....

First drawing

What school does your child belong to: "scribbling in just one corner" or "throwing paint on the canvas"? Does he love all the colors of the rainbow or stick to one palette? Is he more of a Claude Monet or a Jackson Pollock?

When did your child draw for the first time?

....

....

What did he use to create her masterpiece?

....

....

What did it look like? ....

....

....

Who was it for? ....

....

....

What did it show about your child's personality?

....

....

....

....

....

....

Add your child's first drawing here.

First time climbing stairs

More impressive than the Rockies and Mount Everest combined, the top of the staircase is a tempting goal! Your baby was very anxious for those baby gates to come down so she could make her first solo climb . . .

How old was your child? ....

Did she scale the summit without your knowledge, or did you strictly supervise the feat? ....

....

Where was the staircase? ....

Did she climb on all fours or walk up? ....

....

Do the stairs hold a particular fascination for your child? ....

....

If you have stairs, do you have a gate at the bottom or top? ....

....

First tantrum

You should always look at tantrums as your child's way of asserting himself, as the first tantrum is never the last. You'll be dealing with frequent outbursts, cries of frustration, and confrontations. Your little one is no longer a baby and wants to make sure you know it.

How old was your child? ....

Where did it happen? ....

What triggered it? ....

....

What did he do (shriek, kick on the floor)? ....

....

Who else was there? ....

....

How did you react? ....

....

....

First time on the potty

Were you in a hurry to ditch the diapers, or were you the "She'll be ready when she's ready" type? Was your child anxious to start wearing her big girl pants? By the end it's a relief for everyone!

How old was your child? ....

Who wanted to try it first? ....

Did she use a potty seat or go straight for the big toilet? ....

....

How did it go? ....

....

How long did it take your child to become fully potty trained? ....

....

Any funny anecdotes to remember? ....

....

....

First night without a diaper

The long-awaited night has arrived. Like a practiced acrobat, your baby is ready for the big time. You close your eyes and cross your fingers until morning. Drum roll please!

How old was your child? ....

Did he ask, or did you have to convince him?

....

....

Did you use any tricks to prevent bed-wetting?

....

....

....

Was the first night a success? ....

....

....

....

First nursery rhyme

How adorable to hear your child recite a nursery rhyme,
misplaced words and all! Nursery rhymes help your child
learn to talk and offer a chance to connect. Your child will
treasure them and pass them on to her own children.

What nursery rhyme did your child first

remember? ....

....

Where did she learn it? ....

....

When did she first recite it? ....

....

....

Your child's favorite rhymes and stories: ....

....

....

....

First tricycle

What a proud moment when your toddler mounted
that tricycle the first time! Even if he turned a deaf
ear to your earnest cries of "Turn the pedals!" he still
had a blast gripping the handle bars while being pushed
by his loved ones!

How old was your child? ....

What kind of tricycle was it? ....
....

Where was his first ride? ....
....

Did he stay put on the seat? ....
....
....

Was he able to pedal? ....
....
....

First "big kid" birthday party

What a great day! Your child is now old enough to enjoy being the center of attention, while you get to know all of her friends. A day filled with excitement, pressure, and plenty of emotion . . .

How many candles did your child blow out?

....

What day was the big event? ....

Where was it held? ....

....

Who was there? ....

....

What were the activities? ....

....

....

What gifts did your child receive? ....

....

Jot down some anecdotes and stories: ....
....
....
....
....
....

Add an invitation here.

First time getting dressed alone

Underpants on backward, shirt inside out, and buttons in the wrong holes . . . that doesn't stop your child from smiling proud at this big accomplishment! Just another step on the long road to independence, a journey fraught with such perils as zippers and shoelaces!

How old was your child? ....

....

Was his reaction "I can do it myself!" or "Why won't you do it?" ....

....

....

....

Did he like to pick out his own clothes? ....

....

....

....

First favorite outfit

Now that your child can dress herself (or maybe even before then!), she has a favorite outfit that you just can't get her to take off. She plays in it, sleeps in it, wears it all day every day. You find it impossible to keep clean!

How old was your child? ....

What did the outfit look like? ....
....

Why did she like that particular clothing so much?
....
....

Did she wear it anywhere unusual? ....
....

How did you finally convince her to change
outfits? ....
....
....

First night in a "big kid" bed

The crib that kept your wee one snug and safe those first years is now too small. It's time to change to a big bed: a symbol of freedom and independence.

How old was your child when he made the switch to a big bed? ....

Was he excited or nervous? ....
....

Did you get a bed with rails? ....

How did the change affect him those first few nights? ....
....

Did the transition change anything in your routine? ....
....
....

First favorite movie or show

Even if you try not to let your child spend too much time in front of the television, sometimes you're in awe at the peace and quiet you can get when your child's favorite movie or show is on . . . although you do get tired of hearing those same songs over and over.

What was your child's favorite movie or show?

....

How old was she when she first saw it? ....

What's the record for the number of times she watched it in a row? ....

What were her favorite things about it? ....

....

....

Did she have any other favorite movies or shows?

....

....

First stick figure

One day, your child's mass of messy lines on the
paper gives shape to a cute but alien-like stick figure!

Does your child's figure look more like a creation
from Picasso (dynamic with limbs everywhere),
Matisse (showing a love for the basics), or Haring
(full of color and movement)? ....

....

Who taught your child to draw figures? ....

....

Add your child's first
stick figure drawings here.

First day at school

Just yesterday, he was learning to hold his bottle by himself, and here you are taking him to his first day of school. Your child has made so much progress!

What was the date? ....

What was the name of the school? ....
....

Were there tears (from you, or your child)? ....
....

What was the teacher's name? Was there a
teaching assistant? ....
....

What did your child bring to school (favorite toy,
snack, books)? ....
....

How did the first day go? ....
....

First "signature"

Maybe her lines overlap or sprawl across the page in wavy letters (that are sometimes backward) but who cares! It's a joy to see your child write her first name with her own little hand! What a fantastic keepsake . . .

How old was your child? ....

Where did she make her first writing attempt (at school or at home)? ....

....

....

> Add one of your child's
> first drafts here.

First school field trip

The first field trip is exciting, whether it's a quick walk to a neighborhood park or a bus ride to the local museum. You have to prepare your child's gear, get his backpack ready, and make sure nothing's forgotten! You probably reminded him a million times to listen to the teacher and not wander off . . .

Where was your child's first field trip? ....

....

Did you chaperone? ....

What were your child's reactions? ....

....

....

....

Jot down some anecdotes and memories: ....

....

....

....

....

First time on stage

Since birth, your child has been the star of your family's show. Then one day, she got up on stage in front of an entire audience to show off her fantastic personality . . . from your objective view, of course!

When was the first time she was in a performance?

....

What was her role? ....

....

Was she anxious about being in the spotlight?

....

....

How did she handle her first stage experience?

....

....

How did it make you feel? ....

....

....

First trip to the movies

At the movies, everything is larger than life: the screen,
the sound, the seats . . . and your child's emotions! How did
your little one react to this blockbuster experience?
Was he impressed, scared, or captivated?

What was your child's first movie? ....
....

How old was he? ....

Who went with him? ....

Did he make it through the whole thing without
getting up? ....
....

Did your child like the movie? ....
....

What did he think of the experience overall?
....
....

First extracurricular activity

One of your child's friends wants to do gymnastics;
another is set on art. A mother you know thinks that
kid's yoga is the next big thing. What activity did you
choose for your child, or did she choose for herself?

What was your child's first extracurricular activity? ....

....

....

....

Who chose the activity? ....

....

....

Why this activity? ....

....

....

....

....

When and where was it held? ....

....

....

....

What was the instructor's name? ....

....

....

Did your child look forward to the class? ....

....

....

....

Did your child stick with this activity, or decide to
try a different one? ....

....

....

....

....

First lost tooth

Losing a tooth is another step in the long process of growing up! The pearly white still rings with the sound of your tot's laughter, but it is now the rightful property of the Tooth Fairy, who will take good care of it.

How old was your child? ....

Which tooth was it? ....

How did the tooth come out? ....

....

....

What was your child's reaction? ....

....

....

What did the Tooth Fairy bring? ....

....

....

First sleepover

When your child is invited to his first sleepover,
his excitement will grow and grow as he packs his bag and
hears your gentle warning of "Don't have too much fun!"
How did things go in the end?

Who hosted the sleepover? ....

How old was your child? ....

Was he anxious at all? ....

....

What did he pack in his overnight bag? ....

....

How did it go with your child? ....

....

Did you sit back and relax, or stress out on your
"night off"? ....

....

....

My Book of Firsts with Sophie la Girafe

Copyright © 2015 The Experiment, LLC

Translation by Amy Butcher

First published in France by Marabout as *Le Journal des premières fois avec Sophie la Girafe* © Hachette Livre, 2014. This revised and updated English-language edition is published by arrangement with Marabout.

© SOPHIE LA GIRAFE All rights reserved
Modèle déposé / Design patent
Sophie la girafe © : Product protected by copyright (by order of the Paris court of appeal dated 30 June 2000)

The Experiment, LLC
220 East 23rd Street, Suite 301
New York, NY 10010-4674
www.theexperimentpublishing.com

This book contains the opinions and ideas of its author. It is intended to provide helpful and informative material on the subjects addressed in the book. It is sold with the understanding that the author and publisher are not engaged in rendering medical, health, or any other kind of personal professional services in the book. The author and publisher specifically disclaim all responsibility for any liability, loss, or risk—personal or otherwise—that is incurred as a consequence, directly or indirectly, of the use and application of any of the contents of this book.

The Experiment's books are available at special discounts when purchased in bulk for premiums and sales promotions as well as for fund-raising or educational use. For details, contact us at info@theexperimentpublishing.com.

ISBN 978-1-61519-290-8

Cover and text design by Marabout

Manufactured in China
Distributed by Workman Publishing Company, Inc.
Distributed simultaneously in Canada by Thomas Allen & Son Ltd.

First printing May 2015
10 9 8 7 6 5 4 3 2 1